The Endless Story
Explaining Life and Death to Children

Melissa Kircher

The Endless Story: Explaining Life and Death to Children
Copyright © 2018 by Melissa Kircher. All rights reserved.

Published by private party.

No part of this book may be reproduced in any form or by any electronic or mechanical means including information storage and retrieval systems, without permission in writing from the author.
The only exception is by a reviewer, who may quote short excerpts in a review.

Requests for reproduction should be addressed via e-mail to: contact@melissakircher.com

For more information visit www.melissakircher.com.

Cover design and layout by Melissa Kircher

Printed in the United States of America

First Printing: May 2018

ISBN-13:
978-1987566543

ISBN-10:
1987566548

To Nora

For asking, "Is everyone going to die?"

& To Sean

For scribbling in red marker all over Mommy's sketchbook while she answered.

One day, you were born.

Every person in the whole world has the same beginning.

We all start life as babies.

We grow taller, wider, smarter, and more fantastic month by month and year by year.

Babies become children,
children become teenagers,
and teenagers become adults.

Adults are kids who are all grown up.

We are adults for a long time.

Then, slowly, over many years, we get older.

Eventually, our hair turns gray.
Our skin gets wrinkles.

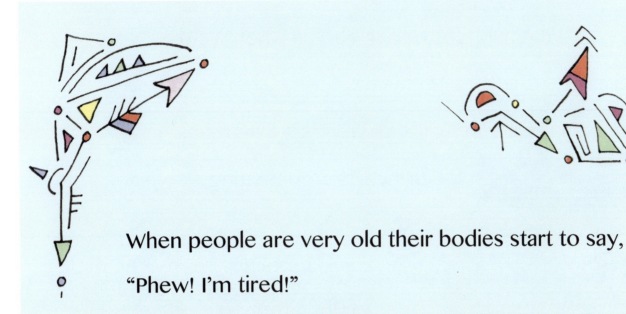

When people are very old their bodies start to say,

"Phew! I'm tired!"

It's time for them to die.

Sometimes, people get sick or have accidents and they die before they are old.

Do you know anyone who has died?

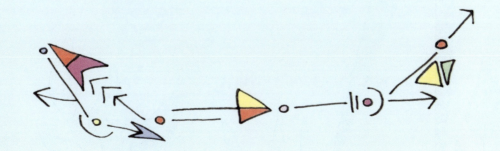

What happens to our bodies when we die?

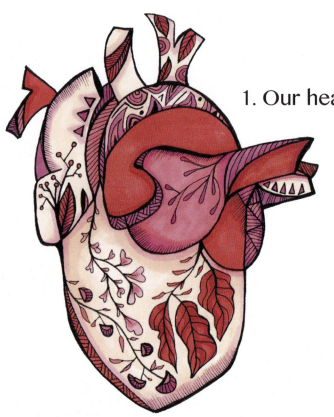

1. Our hearts stop beating.

2. Our lungs stop breathing.

3. Our eyes stop seeing.

4. Our brains stop thinking and telling our bodies what to do.

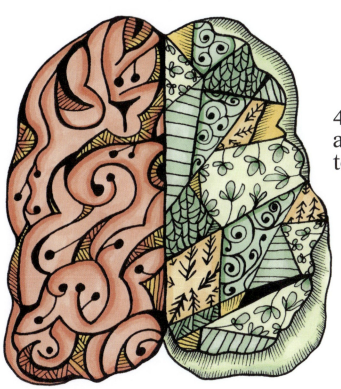

The truth is,
   at some point everything dies.

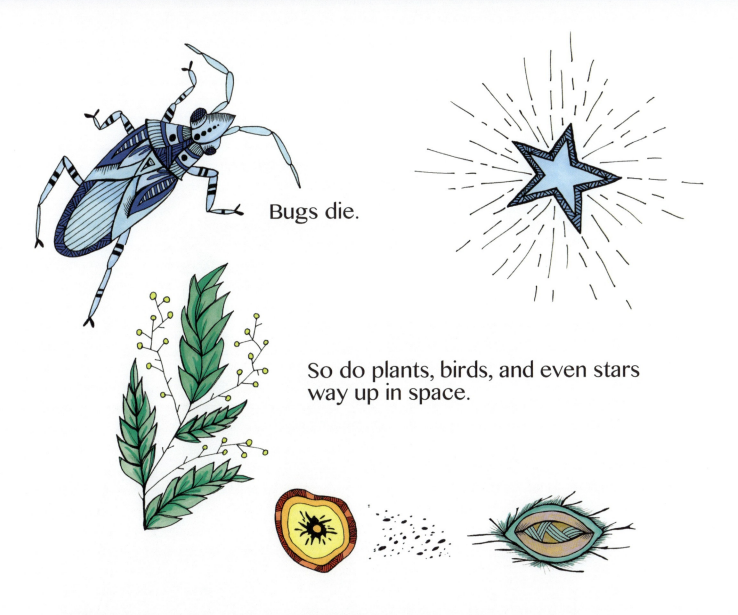

Bugs die.

So do plants, birds, and even stars way up in space.

There are teeny, tiny cells that we can only see under a microscope and they die, too.

Everything in the whole universe dies, but death is not the end of our stories.

Lots of cultures bury their loved ones in the ground after they die. Families put up gravestones to mark the important spot.

Sometimes, bodies are burned and the ashes are scattered in special places like the ocean, a forest, or on top of a mountain.

We become part of the Earth again.

Science shows us that dead cells and dead bodies decay and then transform into new things like:

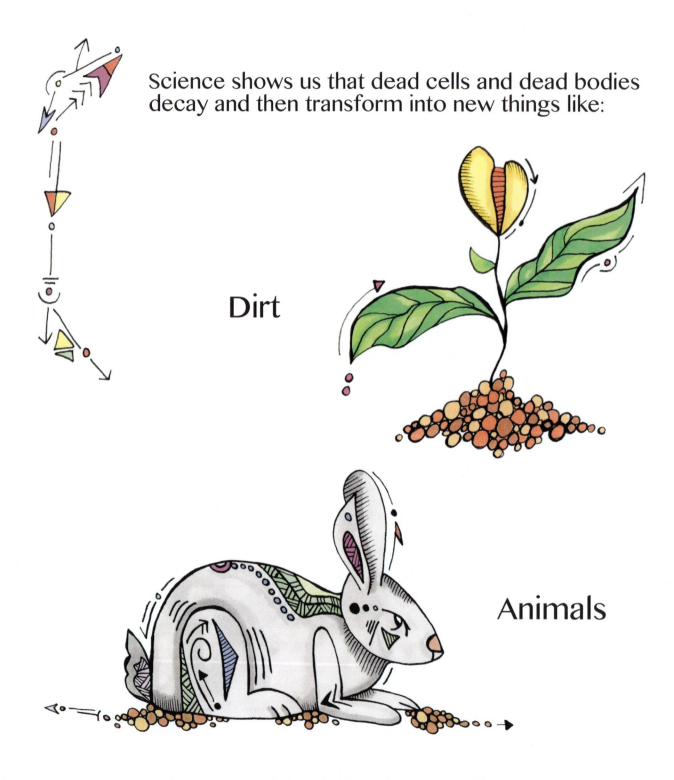

Dirt

Animals

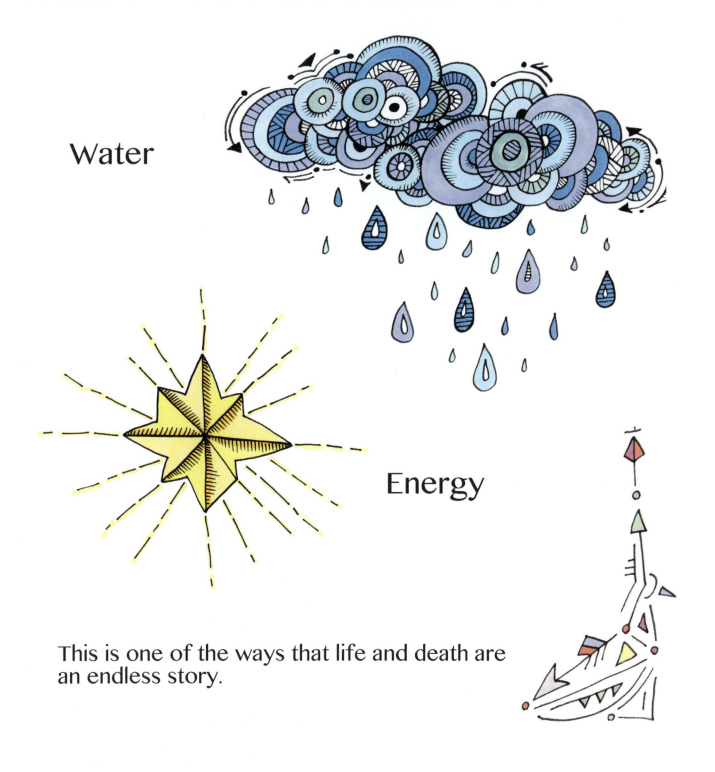

Water

Energy

This is one of the ways that life and death are an endless story.

Talking about death might make us feel sad or scared.

This is okay.

It helps to cry or ask for a hug.

Sometimes, we feel just fine talking about death — and that's okay, too!

But what happens to US when we die?

What happens to the parts of us that love banana sandwiches, coloring, and going to the beach? What happens to our thoughts, feelings, and memories?

Many people believe that every person has a soul. A soul is like the wind, you can't see it, but it's real. It's what makes you... you!

Our bodies die, but our souls live on as part of the endless story.

There are all kinds of ideas about what happens to our souls after we die.

Some cultures believe souls are reborn into new people or animals.

They call this reincarnation.

Others believe our souls go to a place with no pain or suffering called heaven. In heaven people who have died are reunited with the souls of their loved ones and with God.

Some believe our souls become part of nature — Mother Earth.
We make up one Great Spirit of all things.

And still others think our souls
rise up and become stars.

What does your family believe about what
happens after death? Why do they believe this?

When people or animals die we miss them.

We love them and wish they could
be on earth with us forever.

But, can I tell you a secret?

Love is another reason that death isn't the end of the story.

Love is passed down from family to family,
from friend to friend, person to person —

Love never dies.

So, how can we love and remember people who have died?

We think about the adventures we had or funny jokes we shared.

We tell stories about them or draw pictures of them.

We can ask someone to show us photographs of them while they were alive.

We can visit their favorite places or eat their favorite foods.

What does your family do to honor people who have died?

Dying is part of life.

It's cool and sad and interesting and a little scary.

Being alive right now means we're part of the endless story.

The story of life and death and science and soul and love — the story that goes on forever.

Maybe it's time for another hug.

Printed in Poland
by Amazon Fulfillment
Poland Sp. z o.o., Wrocław